Celebrate Together

Preparing for the First Communion Mass

REJOICE PUBLICATIONS

Celebrate Together

Preparing for the First Communion Mass

Marie Connolly
Maureen Knight
Peter McGrail
Ellie McKeown

Illustrations and photographs by John Callaghan

Acknowledgements

The authors would like to thank the many people in the Archdiocese of Liverpool who helped in the development of this publication.

We would like to thank the Department for Christian Education and the Department for Pastoral Formation in the Archdiocese of Liverpool for their support throughout the development of *Celebrate Together*, in particular Rev Desmond Seddon, Rev David Melly, Sr Teresa Flynn, Ms Nora Finnegan, Mr Paul Mannings and Ms Pauline Milsom.

We are most grateful to those parishes in the Archdiocese of Liverpool who trialled the material and gave such encouraging feedback. Finally, heartfelt thanks to our families especially Jack and Mary Fleming for sharing their lifetime of "celebrating together" with us.

Published by Rejoice Publications
an imprint of
Matthew James Publishing Ltd
19 Wellington Close
Chelmsford
Essex CM1 2EE
www.matthew-james.co.uk

ISBN 1 899481 26 5

First published in 2005

Nihil obstat: George Stokes, Censor
Imprimatur: Rt Rev Thomas McMahon, Bishop of Brentwood
Brentwood 15 April 2005

Design by Gill England
Printed by Gallpen, Norwich, England

Contents

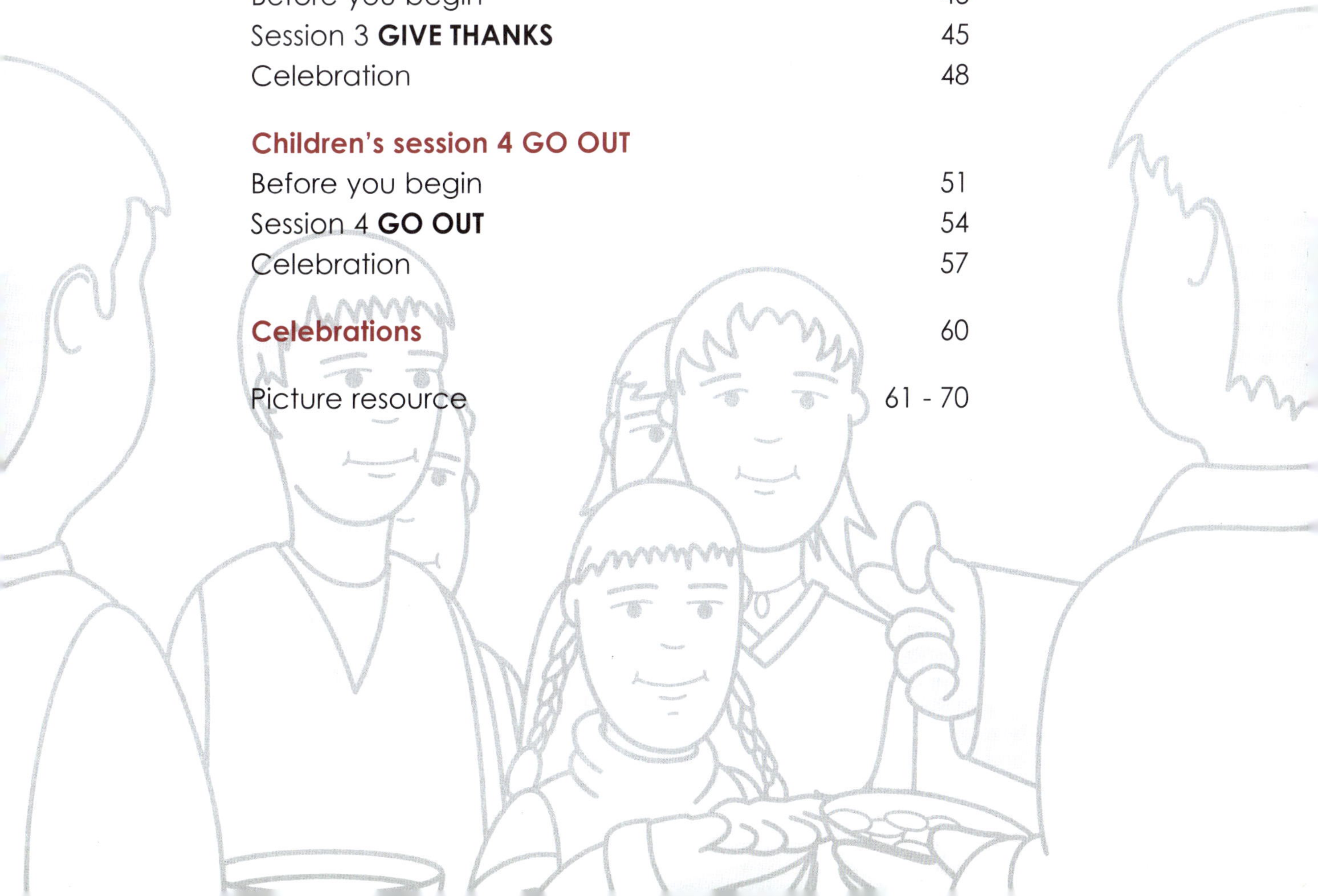

Foreword

As Chair of the Steering Committee for 'Living and Sharing Our Faith – a national Project for Catechesis and Religious Education', and as President of the National Board of Religious Inspectors and Advisers I am very pleased to welcome 'Celebrate Together – a resource for liturgical catechesis'.

The Primary Religious Education Advisers and the Parish Catechetical Advisers for the Archdiocese of Liverpool have worked collaboratively and extensively to bring you this excellent and attractive resource to enhance and enrich your parish preparation for the celebration of the First Communion Liturgy.

The Advisers were influenced by the content of *On the Threshold (1)* which challenged all those involved in Catechesis and Religious Education to consider the reality of the situation in which Christian initiation takes place. The Advisers recognised the need to acknowledge the true understanding of and participation in the Sunday Liturgy by some 'less active' families.

The result is *Celebrate Together* which offers parents and children an understanding of the Sunday Mass Celebration based upon key people, places, symbols and phrases. It is not intended as a 'stand alone' programme. It assumes the fuller preparation of the children for the reception of First Eucharist through school – and parish-based programmes. It is a 'final stage' resource which aims to prepare children and their parents for the First Communion Mass celebration in a welcoming and accessible form.

I consider *Celebrate Together* represents an innovative and realistic approach to the interface between the active worshiping community within a parish and the wider community who approach the parish at specific milestones in their journey of faith. In the spirit of *On the Threshold*, this approach enables the parish community to act, not as a 'gatekeeper', but as a 'threshold companion' to all those who come to the parish hoping to celebrate together.

I commend this resource to you and offer my thanks to the Team at the Liverpool Archdiocese Centre for Evangelisation for their dedication to this task.

+Edwin

Bishop of Wrexham

Celebrate Together
Preparing for the First Communion Mass
A Resource for Liturgical Catechesis

The concept

The Resource consists of material to assist final preparation of children for the First Holy Communion liturgy. It reinforces and develops further work done in school through ***Here I Am***, or in the parish through ***Walk With Me***. In that sense, therefore, it cannot be seen as a stand-alone programme. It is, rather, to be understood as **the final element in a process of preparation** that extends from the beginning of the child's primary school life. By focussing this final phase of preparation on the liturgical community, the resource also reinforces the essential partnership of parish, school and home in the formation of the child.

Structure

The Resource consists of three elements:

1 Two meetings with parents. These aim to forge links between the parents' experience of the children's Baptism and the forthcoming First Communion. Key to this is an affirmation of their role as parents and 'first teachers of the faith.'

2 Four catechetical sessions with the children. These are based upon the structure of the Mass. At the heart of each there is a facilitated encounter with a member of the parish who plays a key role in either preparing or celebrating the liturgy. If possible, the children will experience the liturgical space within which their First Communion will take place, and will also gain familiarity with key liturgical items that will feature in their First Communion.

3 Four celebrations for children and parents, led by the catechetical teams. These develop the themes covered in the children's sessions, and may follow on directly from them or take place at a later date.

(An optional panel is available as a supplementary resource. This enables children to share more fully with their parents what has been covered in their sessions.)

The role of the catechist

The parish catechetical team plays a key role throughout the resource. They lead the various sessions, working with parents and children alike, facilitating the children's encounters with various liturgical players, and leading the celebrations that follow on from each of the children's sessions.

The Resource aims to equip parish catechists as fully as possible. Each session (either with parents or children) is preceded by a ***Before you Begin*** section. This may be used initially for personal reflection, and as the format for a preparatory meeting of catechists.

How to celebrate together

The home, school, parish partnership is one in which all partners have distinct yet complementary roles. As children prepare to receive their first Eucharist these partners are called to work together to ensure that those preparing have the richest experience possible for their age and stage of development. To find out more about this partnership it would be helpful to get in touch with your local Catholic primary school.

The Church has always acknowledged parents as the first and most important educators of their children in matters of faith. ***Celebrate Together*** has been developed to help parishes assist parents in this task. ***Celebrate Together*** consolidates and further develops the Sacramental education children receive in school through the ***Here I Am*** programme, or in their parish through ***Walk with Me***. Each year through their religious education in school or catechesis in parish children acquire and build on previous knowledge, understanding and skills in a developmental and progressive manner.

Overview of Sacraments in topics of *Here I am*

- In the Autumn term of each year throughout the primary years, the sacraments of Baptism and Confirmation are explored through one of the followig topics: Invitations, Friends, Initiation, Signs and Symbols.
- In the Spring term, the Sacrament of Eucharist is explored through: Communion, Meals, Memories, Thanksgiving.
- In the Summer term, the Sacrament of Reconciliation is explored through: Choices, Change, Freedom and Responsibility, Building Bridges.

The study of these sacraments, however, is not confined to these topics. For example, in the topic on Self-Giving for Lent, the sacrificial aspect of Eucharist is explored further; the topics on Good and Evil (Lent) and Difference (Universal Church) complement the work done for Reconciliation.

Children learn about the other three sacraments: Anointing the Sick, Holy Orders and Marriage. In topics Celebrations they learn about sacraments as the Church's celebrations of God's gifts and how these mark and make holy the important stages of Christian life.

This deepening of their knowledge and understanding of the Eucharist continues throughout primary school and is further developed in secondary schools where children follow the ***Icons*** programme. Indeed, sacramental education is a lifelong process.

During the last weeks of preparation prior to receiving Eucharist for the first time ***Celebrate Together*** reinforces what children already know, understand and can do in relation to the Sacrament of the Eucharist by providing them with enriching experiences where they meet, work and celebrate with members of their parish and become familiar with the church and the Mass. This preparation is undertaken in a very practical way.

Celebrate Together

Introduction of the Concept

Type of programme

Not to be a stand-alone programme, but to complement the work done;

- in school through ***Here I Am***
- in parishes through ***Walk With Me***

The overall aim

- to prepare parents and children for the liturgical celebration of First Communion.
- therefore, a **FINAL** phase of preparation.

Type of catechesis

- liturgical

Concept

Parents' sessions

- to link celebration of First Communion with the previous significant celebration of their child's Baptism;
- to relate the experience of their own hopes and anxieties for their children.

Children's sessions

- experience of the (liturgical space) where their First Communion will take place (if possible);
- familiarity with key liturgical items that will feature in their First Communion;
- introduction to key people who play a special part in preparing for the celebration of their First Communion Day.

Celebrations (parents and children)

- ideally this would follow the children's session. It is an opportunity for parents and children to celebrate together with the catechist what has been covered in their session.

Aim for the catechists

- to equip as far as possible parish catechists to perform this task.

In brief

- It starts from a recognition that in practical terms the core experience that most of our families have of the parish community is the parish school.
- It aims to facilitate a fruitful encounter between the children and their parents on the one hand and the broader, celebrating community on the other.
- It may be helpful to have an additional meeting with parents to discuss the practical details of the day of celebration.

Before you begin working with parents

Remember that each of the parents will be at a different place in their own journey of faith and in their relationship with the Church. Your task is not to make assumptions about either of these but rather to create a comfortable and relaxed atmosphere in which they will be able to share some of their experience. Listen carefully to what parents are saying and try to respond with non-judgemental acceptance. In this way you will be able to build up the trust necessary for parents to share honestly their hopes, fears and concerns. This in turn, will hopefully lead to a deeper appreciation of how their story fits into the Christian story.

Before you start you might find it useful to read again the story of the two disciples on the road to Emmaus in Luke's Gospel, chapter 24, verses 13-32. *(See colour picture on page 62)*

As you read, note the following:

- Jesus approaches the disciples and walks silently alongside them for some time; He asks a question and listens as they tell their story;
- Only then does Jesus offer his perspective on the events that have just occurred;
- He exerts no pressure on the disciples. He gives them space to reflect on what they have heard;
- Jesus responds to their invitation to spend more time with them.

How could you follow this pattern in the way that you work with the parents of First Communion children?

Our hope is that you will be able to build relationships that will continue long after the First Communion event is over. For this to happen people ideally need to meet in small, informal groups. This resource can also be used with a large group of First Communion parents provided that they have the opportunity to do the discussion exercises in pairs or small groups. Alternatively, you may decide that it is worth duplicating meetings so that your gatherings can be smaller. You might also think about alternative venues… for instance you might decide to meet in each other's houses. Make sure you are aware of any disabilities within the parent group. Venues should be accessible for all. Also your sessions should be prepared with the level of ability of all participants in mind. It just calls for a few people to get together and think creatively about providing new and varied ways in which parents can have the space and opportunity to reflect on the significance of this special event in their own lives and in the lives of their children.

PARENTS' SESSION 1

Aim: to forge links between the parents' experience of their children's Baptism and the forthcoming First Communion.

Focus: the Post-Baptismal symbols of white garment and candle.

Learning outcome: to better perceive the Catholic Community's appreciation of their role in fostering the unique dignity of their child.

RESOURCES

- children's own illustrations of themselves
- flipchart

DISPLAY

- white christening shawl
- large white candle *(see picture on page 64)*

1 WELCOME AND INTRODUCTION (5 mins)

- Welcome the parents
- Explain who you are – and introduce the other members of the catechetical team.

Explain

- This is the first of two meetings that will introduce them to the sessions for their children and themselves ahead of the First Communion day.
- Today we are going to think about the ways in which each of our children is special.

2 OPENING EXERCISE (5 mins)

- Explain that every parent has inside them a treasury of memories of their children. Sometimes we share these memories with other people – usually by telling a story. Ask the parents to think back over the years of their child's life, and to see if they can think of a story about their child that they tend to share with other people?
- Invite them to share this story with the person sitting next to them.

Feedback (5 mins)

This is not just a case of receiving the story. Ask questions like,

- 'Why is that story special?'
- 'How does it feel to share it with others?'

3 GROUPWORK (10 mins)

Spend time considering the following questions in small groups:

- What are the ways in which each of your children is unique?
- What is it like trying to live in a family where the children are very different from each other.... What is good about it? What is difficult?
- What are the ways in which you make each one know that s/he is special?
- How do you attempt to meet their individual needs without the others experiencing favouritism?

4 INPUT (10 mins)

Take some feedback and emphasise the following points:

Every child is unique

Explain that every child is unique; use an example from your own family (or one you know well) to draw out the very different qualities of the children. Sometimes this uniqueness can make things difficult for you – you may point to the different likes and dislikes that can turn meal times, or TV viewing, or shopping for clothes into a nightmare! And yet each child can bring something different and special to your family life. It is important to each child that he or she knows that you appreciate his/her strengths, that you celebrate achievements, and help each to work through his/her particular difficulties.

Meeting each child's individual needs

And yet there is a tension - parents strive to treat all their children alike. We all want to be able to say 'I have no favourites – I love them all the same.' But helping each one to develop his or her particular strengths, or giving time to help one through a particular problem or difficulty can be mis-read by the others. So we are careful to send out the right signals to them all. (You might be able to give an example from your own experience of how difficult this is, or you may point to practices in society – for example the growing trend for parents to give 'also presents' to a birthday child's brothers and sisters – so that they won't feel left out.) It can often feel like 'walking a tightrope.'

Every child is special on his or her First Communion day

This is one of the things that makes First Communion different. It is one of the rare occasions in the life of your child when you will treat him or her as special – and mark them out. On the day they become the very centre of life in your family.

It is a great opportunity to celebrate their particular gifts, achievements and individuality. And because every child in the family has their First Communion Day, then no-one is left out – 'It will be your turn' to the younger ones, 'Do you remember when...?' to those older. All the family celebrates this child.

The dignity of each of God's children

Something like that also happened at the child's Baptism. Your child wore white garments for the ceremony – most probably you also wrapped her or him in a special white Christening shawl towards the end of the ceremony. For many people those shawls are a bit of a family heirloom – passed on from one generation to the next; they can be a sign that the child 'belongs' within its family. But the colour white also has a special meaning for Christians; it is a sign of the dignity of each of God's children. So, when your child was clothed in white, these words were spoken:

See in this white garment the outward sign of your Christian dignity. With your family and friends to help you by word and example bring that dignity unstained into the everlasting life of heaven.
(taken from rite of Baptism)

5 GROUPWORK (10 mins)

Ask parents to return to their groups and consider these two questions:

- What are you going to do on the First Communion day that will show the child s/he is special?
- What do you want him/her to remember from the day?

Take brief feedback (5 mins)

6 CLOSING REFLECTION (10 mins)

Read the following slowly. It will help to have some music playing quietly in the background.

Each of us wants the best for our children. We want them to grow in the good ways in which they are unique and special (and to grow OUT of any 'special' BAD habits they might have!)

We sometimes can become anxious that we aren't up to this task. Actually, there is no such thing as a 'perfect' parent – we all have 'L' plates stuck to our backs. All parents make mistakes with their children – but what is important is for us to learn from them.

In the same way, the best way we can help our children to grow is to remain open, and to share with them as appropriate the lessons that we have learned during our own lives.

So we share with them the good things that others have passed on to us – the values that were given to us as we grew and which we have held onto, the lessons that we have learned from our own mistakes as life has gone on. We hope that they will be spared making the same mistakes (Actually, as they grow up, they probably make mistakes that we could NEVER have even thought of!) And as they grow – we learn from them!

(Light the candle in the display and continue…)

One of the treasures that we share with them is the faith of the community in which they were baptised. At your child's baptism you received a candle from the Church as a sign of the faith of the Catholic community. Over the years since then part of the 'good things' that you have tried to pass onto your children has been that of faith. A candle is actually a good symbol for faith. Because, when you look at a candle, its flame might appear very fragile, flickering and small. Yet, it always seems to bring just enough light. Our faith can be like that – we often can think that like the candle flame our faith is very small, flickering and weak. Yet, it is always just enough to hold onto – just enough to see us through. You have shared that faith with them in the years up till now. Bringing them now for the First Communion is taking them one step further down the road.

Invite the parents to look at the display. Ask them to remember the things they have said about their child today – about how they are special.

Invite them in silence, to think again about the hopes that each parent has for their child on their First Communion day.

Finish with this prayer

At their baptism,
your daughters and sons were made children of light by Christ.
May they walk always as children of light.
May they keep the flame of faith alive in their hearts,
as they prepare to receive Him for the first time in Holy Communion. Amen.

7 GOODBYES

- Thank everybody for coming.
- Remind them of the date and place of the next meeting.
- Say that if anyone has any questions, they can approach you and the other catechists.

PARENTS' SESSION 2

Aim: to affirm the parents in their experiences as first teachers of the children in the faith.

Focus: the Post-Baptismal anointing.

Learning outcome: to recognise the relationship between the 'everyday' values that the parents seek to share with their children and the participation of all Christians in the three-fold ministry of Christ.

RESOURCES

- flipchart
- tape recorder
- hand-outs

DISPLAY

- baptismal garment and candle (as last time)
- large clear vessel, part-filled with olive oil *(see picture on page 65)*

1 WELCOME AND INTRODUCTION (5 mins)

Welcome the parents and introduce the second session in this way:

- This is the second of two meetings that will introduce the series of special sessions for their children and themselves ahead of the First Communion day.
- When we last met, we thought about the ways in which each of our children is special. Today we look ahead to their future – and we think about the kind of people we hope they will become.

2 OPENING EXERCISE (5 mins)

Brief discussion in pairs

Invite the participants to have a word with the person sitting next to them:

- What hopes and dreams do you have for your children?
- What anxieties do you have about them as you watch them grow up?

Feedback (5 mins)

Write-up the hopes/dreams and anxieties on the flipchart.

3 GROUPWORK (15 mins)

The participants are assigned to groups, each of which is led by a catechist. When the group has settled, the leader introduces the task:

We've seen some of the hopes and dreams that we hold for our children. Behind those dreams and anxieties there lie our own values – there are certain things that we really want to pass onto our children. We have a strong sense of our own responsibility in all of this – and sometimes we can feel that we make a bit of a mess of it. But the odds are that we're not actually making too bad a job of it. Let's think about the ways in which we ourselves learned.

What are the most important things that your parents or grandparents passed onto you? How did you learn them?

- How have those values served you? Why are they important for your life today?

When the group has explored these, go on to consider:

- What values do you want to pass on to your children?
- What practical signs can you see in their lives that these values are taking root?

4 FEEDBACK (5 mins)

Write-up the values that emerge from the groups.

5 INPUT (15 mins)

Introduction

Each of us want the best for our children. This means passing on to them the lessons that we have learned during our own lives. So we share with them the good things that others have passed on to us – the values that were given to us as we grew and which we have held onto, the lessons that we have learned from our own mistakes as life has go on.

This includes the faith of the community in which they have been baptised. This can sound a daunting task – especially as so often we can feel out-of-touch with the Church, or that we are not particularly 'good' Christians ourselves. But in practice is it really so far removed from the day-to-day values that you have identified? Let's think about it.

What are the different ways in which we use oil today?

After your children had been baptised, each of them was smeared on the forehead with holy oil. *(Draw attention to the oil in the display)*

This was a sign that from the day of their baptism and throughout their lives your children would be like Jesus.

So, what were His values?

1 **He cared for people (Give a couple of examples).**
2 **He stood up for truth (Again, try to give an example).**
3 **He prayed and worshipped God.**

So, the values that the Christian family offers to your children are the same.

1 They are called to **care for others** just as he did.

2 They are called to grow up as **people who want to know things the way they really are, and will not live a lie.**

3 They are called not to take anyone for granted. Instead, they should have a sense of wonder and gratitude – **and acknowledge God's loving presence in their lives**.

We share these values with our children right from their birth – usually without thinking about it. We sometimes do it through the words we speak, but more usually our children 'catch' these values from us by copying the ways in which we act. This is because being a follower of Jesus is as much about the way in which we live our ordinary lives as what happens on a Sunday. But it can sometimes be hard to make the link between the two.

6 CLOSING REFLECTION (10 mins)

Light the candle in the display. Play quiet background music.

Reflection

- Invite the participants to remember again the people who passed on to them the values that they try to live by.
- Ask them again to remember the hopes and dreams they have for their children.

Scripture Passage

Luke 18:15-17: *'People were bringing little children to Jesus'*

People were bringing even infants to Jesus that he might touch them; and when the disciples saw it, they sternly ordered them not to do it. But Jesus called for them and said, 'Let the little children come to me, and do not stop them; for it is to such as these that the kingdom of God belongs. Truly I tell you, whoever does not receive the kingdom of God as a little child will never enter it.'

Prayer

God is the source of life and love.
May he always help us to be the best of teachers to our children,
bearing witness to the faith
by what we say and do.
Through Christ Jesus our Lord.
Amen.

7 GOODBYES

Before you begin working with children

These next sections provide parish catechists with a variety of materials to support their work in preparing children for their First Communion celebration.

- **Before you begin** – material to use together prior to working with the children. This will support catechists at their own level to understand what is explored in each session with the children.
- **The children's sessions** – each session includes a story** and 'key' elements, people, phrases, objects and places.
- **Celebrations** – for children, parents and catechists to share together.

**Helpful guidance for use of story with children

A good story well-told 'captures us' – it holds our attention in a most powerful way. Story unites us to the whole human family as part of our life, our culture and our religion, and it acts as a bridge to one another's cultures as we explore the common human themes of love, purpose, loss, destiny etc. Entering into a story is a safe way of facing the truth about ourselves, which can bring us to wholeness and healing. Story has a built in power to renew. Stories carry deep insights which often a child cannot put into words, but which enable him or her to cope with and make sense of a strange and often bewildering world.

When reading or better still telling the stories in ***Celebrate Together*** the pointers below will help catechists:

- know the story well – don't read directly from the book, use it to support the story and where possible share the illustrations;
- be familiar with the skeleton of the story – the beginning, the climax and the end – the time, place, central character(s) and the sequence of events;
- enter into the mood and meaning;
- rehearse the telling;
- consider the language;
- choose pictures, music, sound effects, artefacts, props and actions to accompany your story telling;
- ensure that you are aware in advance of any disabilities within the group so that the story can be communicated in alternative ways if necessary.

Enjoy celebrating together!

Overview of Children's Sessions 1 – 4

The concept of "KEY" elements, people, phrases, objects and places introduced to the children each session enables them to participate in and understand more fully the celebration of the Eucharist.

Session 1 **GATHER**

What we hope to achieve

To know, understand and experience what it means to belong and gather as a parish family to celebrate together.

Introductory Rites

Gathering
Sign of the cross
Welcome

Key person/people
– those who get church ready

Key phrase
– 'The Lord be with you.' 'And also with you.'

Key object – holy water

Key place – font

Session 2 **LISTEN**

What we hope to achieve

To know and understand the importance of listening.
To experience listening to God's word.

Liturgy of the Word

Old Testament reading
Responsorial Psalm
New Testament reading
Acclamation
Gospel reading

Key person/people – reader

Key phrase – 'This is the Word of the Lord.' 'Thanks be to God.'

Key object – lectionary

Key place – lectern and microphone

Session 3 **GIVE THANKS**

What we hope to achieve

To lead the children to an appreciation of what the things we have to give thanks for, and to provide the opportunity to givethanks for the world, for one another and for Jesus.

Preparation of the Gifts/Offering

Liturgy of the Eucharist

Key person/people – priest

Key phrase
– 'Let us give thanks to the Lord our God.'
'It is right to give him thanks and praise.'

Key object – offertory gifts
– bread, wine, money

Key place – altar

Session 4 **GO OUT**

What we hope to achieve

To begin to understand the concept of stewardship.
To recognise those who support us in this task and those whom we can support.

Rite of Communion
Rite of Sending Forth

Key person/people
– Special Minister of Holy Communion

Key phrase – 'Go in peace to love and serve the Lord.' ' Thanks be to God.'

Key object – pyx

Key place – open door

GATHER

Before you begin

Material to be used by catechists prior to Session 1 **GATHER**

What we hope to achieve

To know, understand and experience what it means to belong and gather as parish family to celebrate together.

1 LOOKING AT OUR LIVES

Read the extract about families by Joan Hasler.

> A Japanese husband stood with his wife and their son and daughter on the platform at a meeting.
> In his staccato English he said,
> 'I am father. I am like coconut – hard on the outside – soft inside.
>
> This is mother. She is like peach –
> soft and lovely on the outside – hard inside.
>
> This is son. He is like banana –
> soft outside, soft inside, not straight and very slippery.
>
> This is daughter. She is like chestnut –
> prickly outside and explodes when heated.
>
> But now we are all changed. We make good fruit salad.'

To think about and discuss

Think of your own family.
Think about the different gifts and qualities.
Think of a time when you gathered to celebrate.
What was the occasion?
Who was present?
Who helped prepare the celebration?
What did this involve?
How did the celebration go?

2a LOOKING AT GOD'S WORD

St Paul explains how we all have our own gifts but the important thing is to use these gifts fully as part of one body – the family of God.

Read: 1 Corinthians 12:12-31 *(You will need a copy of the Bible)*

b LOOKING AT OUR RESPONSE

- What is it that makes you feel you belong to your parish?
- How did you get involved in the parish?
- How can we help the children in our parish discover what it means to belong, and how important it is for us to gather and celebrate together?

3 MAKING THE CONNECTIONS

During Session 1 we are going to help the children do this through an exploration of:

- the ministry of the key person(s) – the people who prepare the church e.g. the sacristan, the flower arrangers, the cleaners, the musicians etc.
- the meaning and use of the key object – the holy water, which we use every time we come into church;
- the meaning of the key location – the font, reminding us that we gather as members of God's family though Baptism;
- the meaning of the key phrase – The Lord be with you – and also with you.

Ideas for the display

Cover a small table with a cloth.
Place a variety of containers for holding holy water on the table and a picture of a font.

Children's session 1 **GATHER**

What we hope to achieve

To know, understand and experience what it means
to belong and gather as parish family to celebrate together.

Key person/people – **those who get church ready**

Key phrase – **'The Lord be with you'. 'And also with you.'**

Key object – **holy water**

Key place – **font**

Use pictures from the back of this book to help explore these key elements.

1 WELCOME AND INTRODUCTION (10 mins)

Ice breaker

Briefly get to know each other using an adjective with the same initial of your name e.g. Lovely Lisa, Daring Dawn or each child tells the group something they would really like everyone to know about themselves.

Working around the display

- What can you see on the table?
- What does it remind you of?
- What do you think it is used for?
- Have you ever seen it being used before? When? How?
- Explain the significance of the holy water in the font as we enter the church.

Key person

The catechist should enable the children to question the key person about their role. Write up a list and ask the group who would like to ask the various questions (be aware that some children will prefer not to). Prompt the children where necessary.

Prompt questions for use with the key person(s)

- How did you become involved in the work you do for the church?
- What does your work in church involve?
- Why do you do it?
- What special training did you have?

- What instructions did you need to follow?
- Do you need special equipment? What do you need?
- How often do you do this work – daily, weekly, occasionally?
- Do you enjoy your role?
- Does anybody help you?
- Do you help other people train for this role?

2 ACTIVITIES (20 mins)

STORY ***Get Busy This Christmas*** by Stephen Waterhouse
(Published by Bloomsbury ISBN 0-7475-5579-6)

Synopsis

The penguins love Christmas and can't wait to get busy preparing. Each can use their talents and skills to help get ready for when they gather to celebrate this special occasion.

Making connections between the story and the key person

This shows that everyone in a community has something to offer in order to get ready or prepare for a special occasion.
Each person in a parish has their own talents/skills, which they can use to help get ready for the special gathering and celebration that is the Mass.

Read the story

Questions

- What occasion were the penguins getting ready to celebrate?
- In the story many penguins helped to get ready to celebrate Christmas. What did they do?
- Did everyone help?
- How do you know the penguins enjoyed the celebration?
- Allow childeren to ask any other relevant questions.

3 KEY PERSON (15 mins)

The catechist facilitates the encounter, encouraging the children to ask questions. Use the prompt questions with the children to interview the key person(s).

4 CLOSING DOWN (10 mins)

- Working with the key phrase: 'The Lord be with you'
  Response: 'And also with you'.
- Drawing out the key location – the font
  drawing out key object.

Ask the children if they have heard the key phrase 'The Lord be with you' *and the response* 'And also with you'.

This phrase reminds us that God is always with us to be our help, guide and support.

Celebration to follow Session 1 **GATHER**

1 GATHERING (5 mins)

- Welcome the parents as they join the children.
- Gather the parents and children around the Baptismal font.
- Welcome them and make sure everybody has a place and is comfortable.
- Song: e.g. 'Come before God' *(Rejoice One, No. 7)*

Catechist: The Lord be with you.

All: **And also with you.**

Recap the children's session.

Key questions

- We listened to a story – can anyone tell us what it was about?
- Who was the special person we met during our session? What do they do?
- What was the special object we looked at? What is it for? Who uses it?

2 SCRIPTURE READING (10 mins)

Introduce: Our special person has a very special job (specify what that is – e.g. for cleaners – to make sure that when people come here to church they find it clean and welcoming – the kind of special place that they would want to come to). Now we are going to listen to a story about how Jesus sent two of his friends to get the room ready for their special Passover Meal.

Light the Gospel Candle

Sing an Alleluia song e.g. 'Halle, halle, halle'; or 'Pass it On!' *(Rejoice One, 71))*

Read 'Holy Thursday' from *God's Story 3*, p.114, based on Mark 14:12-16

Jesus' disciples asked him, 'Where do you want us to go and prepare the Passover Meal for you?' So he sent two of his disciples, saying to them, 'Go into the city. A man carrying a jug of water will meet you there. Follow him to the house he enters. Say to the owner of that house, "The Master says, where is the room were my disciples and I will eat the Passover Meal?" He will show you a large upstairs room all prepared and furnished with couches. Get everything ready for us there.'

The disciples left, went into the city and found everything just as Jesus had told them. They prepared the Passover Meal.

This is the Word of the Lord.
R. Thanks be to God

Sing the Alleluia song again.

Did you know?

Jewish people celebrate a Passover Meal once a year. It reminds them of the time years ago when their ancestors shared a meal together before hurriedly leaving their home, because God was making them His people.

Discussion

- Do you know what the Passover Meal was?
- When did Jesus have this special meal with his friends?
- How would the disciples recognise the man they were going to meet? What would he be carrying?
- Why would people in Jesus' time have water ready to welcome guests?
- Where would you find water in our church?
- What other things have to be got ready when people are gathering for a special meal?

Explanation

- On the day you were baptised, blessed water was poured over you, to show that you were being welcomed into Jesus' family.
- We remember that every time we come into church – does any one know how? What do we always do when we come into church? Do we do something with water?
- Explain the way we use holy water when we come into church – to remind ourselves of our baptism – to show that we are welcome here in God's house when we gather with God's family.

3 REFLECTION (5 mins)

Let's gather ourselves together, make ourselves still, close your eyes if it helps you.

Listen very, very carefully. *(pause)*

We can hear (the traffic outside, the wind/rain, birds singing, the clock ticking etc)

But if we listen very, very hard we can hear some other things – so really listen carefully. *(pause)*

We can hear ourselves – we are not saying anything, and we are keeping very still. But we are still making a very gentle sound – we are breathing in and out. Listen hard to the sound you make as you breathe. *(pause)*

If you listen carefully – now you will hear each other breathing in and out too. *(pause)*

It is a nice sound – because it shows that we are not on our own. That is why it is good to come here to church – because we are never on our own when we come to Mass. There are lots of people here who want to make us feel welcome – people like Mr/Miss/Mrs X *(today's special person)* and Fr. Y. *(pause)*

Whilst everyone still has their eyes closed, say:

> God our Father,
> Thank you for making us welcome in your house.
> Thank you for all the people who work hard to make it a welcoming place.
> Help us to always feel at home here.
> Amen.

Tell everyone they can open their eyes now.

4 GOODBYES

- Thank everybody for coming along.
- Remind them of the date of the next session.
- Say that the catechists will stay on to answer any questions that people might have.
- Give out the optional panels (if appropriate).

LISTEN

Before you begin

Material to be used by Catechists prior to Session 2 **LISTEN**

What we hope to achieve

To know and understand the importance of listening.
To experience listening to God's word.

1 LOOKING AT OUR LIVES

Think of all the different opportunities we have for listening in our own lives.

Share them with the group e.g. the radio, television, children's stories from school, gossip etc.

Listen to some reflective music together. Make yourselves comfortable, close your eyes if this helps, and breath in and out slowly.

Give the group an opportunity to relax and listen to their own breathing pattern.
'What do you hear?'

Ask the catechists to listen as you read the extract from Documents Catechetiques

'God speaks very gently to children, often without words, the natural creation provides the vocabulary, leaves, clouds, flowing water, a shaft of light. It is a secret language, not to be found in books. One sees a child pause suddenly in the midst of some activity, brought to a silent contemplation of some natural object or living creation or picture.
Here is the quality of looking and listening which brings the child close to God, invoking in one act both the concreteness and the mystery of the world of things. The task of the catechist is to go beyond the admiration of the poet and the question of the philosopher as to the *how* of things and allow the child to find the bond linking him or her with the *who*, God the Creator.'

Documents Catechetiques

To think about and discuss

We all listen but the words we hear may convey something different to each one of us.
What did the extract say to us?
What implications are there for catechists?

Think of your own family. Think about times when you listen to each other.

Do we hear what they are saying?
Do we always listen as carefully as we should?
What stops us from listening to what others are saying to us?

2a LOOKING AT GOD'S WORD

Read: Luke 4:14-22

Jesus came to Nazareth where he had been brought up and went into the synagogue as he usually did. He stood up to read. He was given the scroll of the prophet Isaiah. He unrolled the scroll and found the place and read:

"The spirit of the Lord is upon me for he has chosen me to bring good news to the poor, to heal the broken hearted. He has sent me to set free all those who are imprisoned or oppressed in any way".

He rolled up the scroll, gave it back to the synagogue attendant and sat down.
All the people in the synagogue were looking at him as he said to them
"This passage of scripture came true today while you heard it being read". Everyone was impressed by him and marvelled at the wonderful and powerful words that he spoke.

This is the word of the Lord.
R. Thanks be to God.

b LOOKING AT OUR RESPONSE

What is God's word saying to us?
Do we respond to God's call?
How can we help the children in our parish to listen to and hear God's word?
How important is it for us to gather and listen together?
How do you feel if you are unable to hear for any reason?

3 MAKING THE CONNECTIONS

During Session 2 we are going to help the children make the connections through an exploration of:

- the ministry of the key person(s) – the people who read/proclaim the word of God e.g. the deacon, priest, readers, etc.
- the meaning and use of the key object – the Lectionary, which is used during the Liturgy of the Word in every Mass;
- the meaning of the key location – the lectern (microphone - so that everyone can hear) – the place where the Lectionary rests;
- the meaning of the key phrase – 'This is the Word of the Lord' and the response 'Thanks be to God'.

Hopefully provision will be made in your parish for those who are hearing impaired. You will need to bear this in mind during the session with children, if necessary.

Ideas for the display

Cover a small table with a cloth. Place a Lectionary and a Bible on the table. You may wish to place a microphone on the table as well. Have some photographs of various people reading in church.

Children's Session 2 **LISTEN**

What we hope to achieve

To know and understand the importance of listening.
To experience listening to God's word.

Key person/people – **reader**

Key phrase – **'This is the Word of the Lord.' 'Thanks be to God.'**

Key object – **lectionary**

Key place – **lectern and microphone**

Use pictures from the back of this book to help explore these key elements.

1 WELCOME AND INTRODUCTION (10 mins)

Icebreaker Chinese whispers

Gather the children together in a circle. Start by welcoming them. Introduce them to the theme. See how well they listen. Start off by whispering a message to the first child in the circle to your left. Ask each child to pass on the message to the person next to them, after they have received it until it returns to you. Is it the same message? What does this tell us about our listening skills?

Working around the display:

- What is here?
- What is the difference between the two books?
- Have you seen either of these books before? Where?
- Who reads from a Lectionary?
- Have you ever seen it being used before? When? By whom?

Did you know?

The Lectionary contains the readings that are used at Mass and other celebrations in church. All these readings are taken from the Bible. The different readings are arranged in the Lectionary in the order in which they are used in Mass.
In this way it is easy to find the readings which are most appropriate to the day or celebration.

Key person

Explain who the visitor (key person) will be: What kind of questions would they like to ask them?

The catechist should write up a list and ask the group who would like to ask the various questions (be aware that some children will prefer not to). Prompt the children where necessary.

Prompt questions for use with the key person:

- How did you become involved in the work you do?
- Why do you do it?
- Did you have special training?
- What instructions do you need to follow?
- How often do you do this work – daily, weekly, occasionally?
- Do you enjoy your role?
- What is the name of the book you read from?
- What is in the book?
- Who wrote the book?
- How heavy is the book? (Let the children hold the book)
- Are there any pictures in it?
- Are all Lectionaries the same?
- Are there any other books used during Mass? Who uses them?
- Do you have a favourite reading?

2 ACTIVITIES (20 mins)

STORY ***Not Now, Bernard*** by David McKee
(published by Red Fox ISBN 0-09-924050-5)

Synopsis

The story is about Bernard who has something important to tell his family. There is a monster in his garden. The family is too busy to listen to Bernard. The monster eats Bernard and continues to live in the house. No one appears to notice the difference!

Making the connections between story and the key person

This story shows the importance of listening. When we take someone/something for granted we don't always appreciate the importance of what they are saying to us. We don't always hear. When we are familiar with the readings in church we don't always think about their message.

We should listen carefully and hear what is being said.

Read the story

Questions

- What was Bernard trying to do in the story?
- What happened to Bernard?
- Why did no one notice what had happened?
- Why do you think it is important to listen?

3 KEY PERSON (15 mins)

The catechist facilitates the encounter, encouraging the children to ask questions. Use the prompt questions with the children to interview the key person.

Use the prompt questions for use with the key person.

The key person (the reader) should introduce the children to the key phrase, and location.

4 CLOSING DOWN (10 mins)

- working with the key phrase: "This is the Word of the Lord."
  "Thanks be to God."
- drawing out the key location

Go to church and let the children stand behind the lectern and read from the lectionary using the microphone. Read a short piece of scripture and use the key phrase to conclude.

Celebration to follow Session 2 **LISTEN**

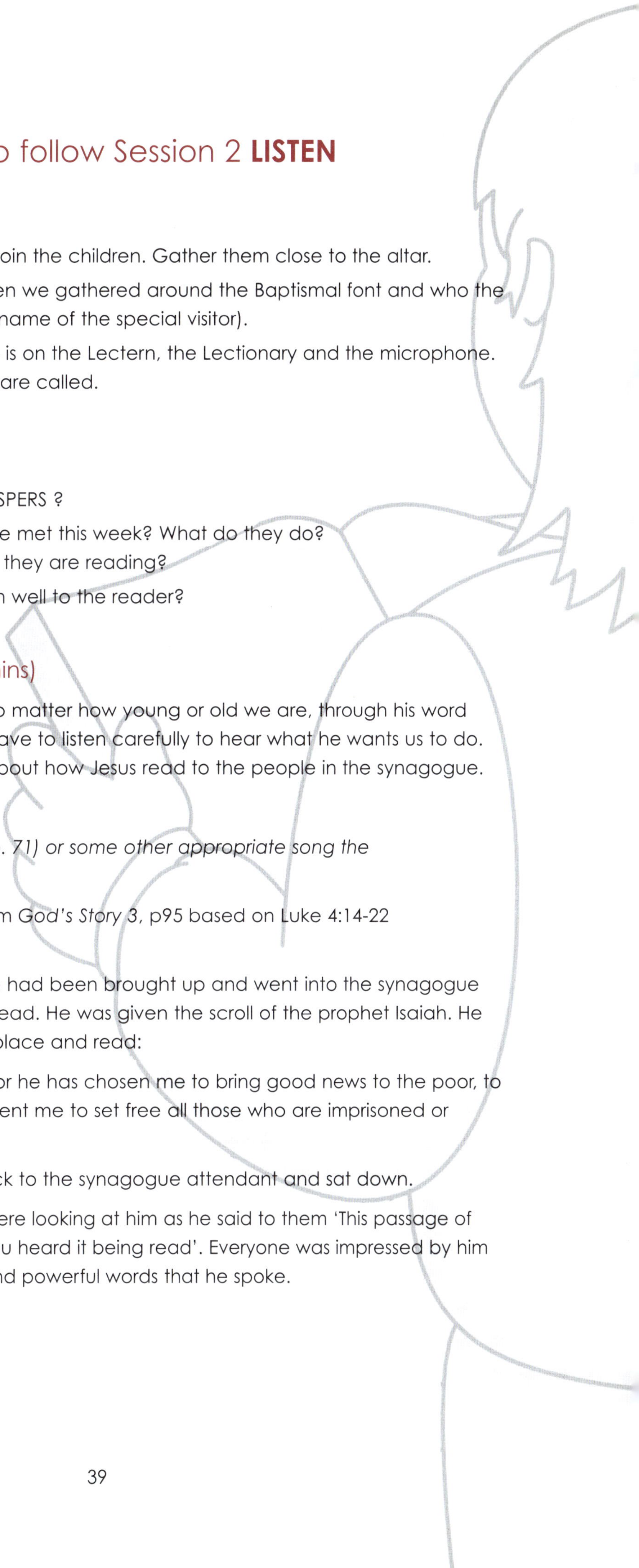

1 GATHERING (5 mins)

- Welcome the parents as they join the children. Gather them close to the altar.
- Recall the last celebration when we gathered around the Baptismal font and who the Special Visitor was (Recall the name of the special visitor).
- Point out that this week's focus is on the Lectern, the Lectionary and the microphone. Point out what different things are called.

Recap the children's session

- Why did we play CHINESE WHISPERS ?
- Who was the special person we met this week? What do they do? What do we have to do when they are reading?
- Why do we have to really listen well to the reader?

2 SCRIPTURE READING (10 mins)

Introduce: God speaks to us all, no matter how young or old we are, through his word which is in the special book. We have to listen carefully to hear what he wants us to do. We are going to listen to a story about how Jesus read to the people in the synagogue.

Light the Candle

Sing 'Pass it On!' *(Rejoice One, No. 71) or some other appropriate song the children know.*

Read 'Jesus begins his mission' from *God's Story 3*, p95 based on Luke 4:14-22
Invite the special person to read.

Jesus came to Nazareth where he had been brought up and went into the synagogue as he usually did. He stood up to read. He was given the scroll of the prophet Isaiah. He unrolled the scroll and found the place and read:

'The spirit of the Lord is upon me for he has chosen me to bring good news to the poor, to heal the broken hearted. He has sent me to set free all those who are imprisoned or oppressed in any way.'

He rolled up the scroll, gave it back to the synagogue attendant and sat down.

All the people in the synagogue were looking at him as he said to them 'This passage of scripture came true today while you heard it being read'. Everyone was impressed by him and marvelled at the wonderful and powerful words that he spoke.

This is the word of the Lord.
R. Thanks be to God

Sing the Alleluia song again.

Did you know?

The synagogue was the meeting-house for the local Jewish community, where they gathered to pray and to listen to the Word of God.

The Word was written by hand on special scrolls. These were treated with great respect and care.

Discussion

Who did the reading in this story?
What did he read from?
Where did he stand?
How did the people in the synagogue react to Jesus' reading?
Have you seen anything like this happen in Church?

Explanation

At Mass, the reader goes to the lectern, the special place from which to read.
The readings are in the special book we call the lectionary.
The reader uses a microphone so that we can all hear the Word of the Lord.
We listen carefully, and try to understand what these words mean to us.
At the end of the reading the reader says 'This is the Word of the Lord' and we say 'Thanks be to God'.

3 REFLECTION (5 mins)

Let's be still for a few moments and think about all that we have heard today, and about how we have listened to each other and to God speaking to us.

What's the best thing you have heard today?

Let's give thanks for all the people who read in church, the people who share God's Word with us.

God our Father,
Listening is a great gift that you,
and all the people in our lives can give us.
We pray for our family, friends and teachers
who listen to us
and we give thanks to you God
our loving Father who always listens.

4 GOODBYES

- Thank everybody for coming along.
- Remind them of the date of the next session.
- Say that the catechists will stay on to answer any questions that people might have.
- Invite children to share panel with parents (if appropriate).

GIVE THANKS

Before you begin

Material to be used by catechists prior to Session 3 **GIVE THANKS**

What we hope to achieve

To lead the children to an appreciation of the things we have to give thanks for, and to provide the opportunity to give thanks for the world, for one another and for Jesus.

1 LOOKING AT OUR LIVES

Play some restful music. Light some candles. Make yourselves comfortable.

Read the poem 'Our World' (Anon)

Our World

Think of a time when you saw the world as beautiful
Think of a sunset over a hill
Or a sunrise on a sleeping city,
Think of a running river or stars shining on a dark sea,
Think of light flashing on a puddle,
a secret quiet place filled with that blue of bluebells,
Think of the vast darkness of a sky studded with a million stars,
Think of a time when you saw the world as beautiful
And give thanks.

Think of a time when you felt pleasure in your body and give thanks,
Think of walking in the wind or planting a flower,
Think of snowflakes falling on your face
Think of the long, slow quiet of summer evenings
and the mystery of moonlight,
Think of morning birdsong, the smell of fresh cut grass,
Think of paddling in the sea or hugging one you love,
Think of the joy of water, a tiny kitten, the first snowdrop, your mother,
Think of a time you were happy in your body – and give thanks.

To think about and discuss

- What is most important in our lives?
- If we were to lose what is most important how would we feel?
- What opportunities do we create for thanking each other and God?

2a LOOKING AT GOD'S WORD

Listen to this reading from Luke 17: 11-19 The curing of the leper.

On the way to Jerusalem Jesus was going through the region between Samaria and Galilee. As he entered a village, ten lepers approached him. Keeping their distance, they called out, saying, "Jesus, Master, have mercy on us!" When he saw them, he said to them, "Go and show yourselves to the priests." And as they went, they were made clean. Then one of them, when he saw that he was healed, turned back, praising God with a loud voice. he prostrated himself at Jesus' feet and thanked him. And he was a Samaritan. Then Jesus asked, "We're not ten made clean? But the other nine, where are they? Was none of them found to return and give praise to God except this foreigner?" Then he said to him, "Get up and go on your way; your faith has made you well."

What does it tell us about giving thanks?
How well do we use gifts, talents, and skills?
How do we appreciate the gift of our world?

b LOOKING AT OUR RESPONSE

What do we want to give thanks for?
How can we help the children in our parish appreciate what is good in their lives?
What opportunities can we provide for them to give thanks for the world, for one another and for Jesus? How can we help them do this during Mass.

3 MAKING THE CONNECTIONS

During Session 3 we are going to help the children do this through an exploration of:

- The ministry of the key person(s) – the priest
- The meaning of the key location – the altar
- The meaning of the key phrase – "Let us give thanks to the Lord our God" – "It is right to give him thanks and praise."
- The key objects – the gifts brought up at the offertory – bread, wine, envelopes etc.

Ideas for the display

Cover a small table with a cloth. Place hosts on a paten, wine in a jug, a basket with parish collection money and envelopes and any other gifts that are brought to the altar regularly, on the table.

Children's Session 3 **GIVE THANKS**

What we hope to achieve

To lead the children to an appreciation of the things we have to give thanks for, and to provide the opportunity to give thanks for the world, for one another and for Jesus.

Key person/people – **priest**

Key phrase – '**Let us give thanks to the Lord our God.**'
'**It is right to give him thanks and praise.**'

Key object – **offertory gifts – bread, wine, money**

Key place – **altar**

Use pictures from the back of this book to help explore these key elements

1 WELCOME AND INTRODUCTION (10 mins)

Icebreaker

It may be possible to use a video extract or photographs here to show some of the wonders of our world e.g. new born babies, waves crashing, snow-capped mountains, the earth from space etc.

You will find suitable material in the God's Story resources pack available from Matthew James Publishing.

Working around the display

- Have you seen a table set like this before? When? Where?
- What do you think it is used for?
- Why is it important to say thank you?
- How do these gifts help us to give thanks?
- Who are the different people to whom we need to say thank you?

Did you know?

Whenever we give a gift we are giving ourselves.
The gifts we take to the altar are ways in which we say thank you to God by giving a little of ourselves. During the consecration we remember Jesus giving himself for us.

Key person

Explain who the visitor (key person) will be i.e. the priest: What kind of questions would the children like to ask him?

Prompt questions for use with the key person.

How long have you been a priest?
What made you decide to become a priest?
How much time does it take?
What is involved? What are your main duties?
Do you need special equipment? What do you need?
Do you get time off?
Do you enjoy being a priest?
Do you need special clothes?
During the mass who carries the gifts?
What are the gifts? (Hosts, wine, collection, any other gifts)
Are they always the same?
Why are these gifts chosen?
Where do they come from?
Who makes them?
What do they taste like?
What happens to them?

2 ACTIVITIES (20 mins)

STORY ***Badger's Parting Gifts*** by Susan Varley
(Published by Picture Lions ISBN 0-00-664317-5)

Synopsis

When Badger dies his friends think they will be sad forever. Gradually they are able to remember Badger with joy, and treasure the gifts he left behind for every one of his friends.

Making Connections between the story and the key person

This story tells us about gifts freely given, and the sense of loss when the gift giver leaves. Jesus gave himself freely to us and left us the gift of himself in the Eucharist, to share together.
For this gift and all our gifts we give thanks.

Read the story

Key questions

What happened to Badger?
How did Badger's friends feel when they realised he had gone?
What helped Badger's friends overcome their grief?
What important thing did Mole do at the end of the story?

3 KEY PERSON (15 mins)

The catechist facilitates the encounter, encouraging the children to ask questions

The key person (the priest) should introduce the children to the key phrase "Let us give thanks to the Lord our God. It is right to give him thanks and praise" and the key location the altar.

- Discuss with children what they would like to give thanks for.
- On a large sheet of paper prepare a litany of thanks or make thank you cards.

For ....
We praise and thank you God.
For ....
We praise and thank you God.
For ....
We praise and thank you God.
For ....
We praise and thank you God.
For ....
We praise and thank you God.
For ....
We praise and thank you God.

Ask each child to either write or draw in a space what he/she wants to say thank you for. This litany or the thank you cards could then become one of the gifts taken up to the altar at their celebration.

Celebration to follow Session 3 **GIVE THANKS**

1 GATHERING (5 mins)

- Welcome the parents as they join the children.
  Gather around the table where the offertory gifts are set out.
- Recall last session.
- We have been talking this week about all the things we are thankful for in our lives and we are especially thankful that you are here with us.

Recap the children's session

- Who was our story about today? What was his name?
- What happened to Badger? How did his friends feel?
- Did they carry on feeling that way?
- How did they change?
- Who was our special visitor this week?
- What did Father say about these special objects on the table.

2 SCRIPTURE READING

Introduce: We are going to hear a very familiar story now about Jesus. Jesus wanted us to remember him always so he did some special things and he told his friends what to do to help us remember him.

Light the Gospel Candle

Sing an Alleluia song e.g. 'Halle, halle, hall' or 'Pass it On!' *(Rejoice One, No. 71)*

Read 'The Last Supper' from *God's Story 3*, p114 based on Mark 14:22-25

In the evening Jesus and the twelve came to supper room.

During the meal Jesus took some bread, blessed it and gave it to them,

'Take this,' he said, 'This is my body'

then he took a cup of wine, said the blessing and gave it to them and they all drank from the cup. He said to them, 'This is my blood, the blood of the covenant, which will be poured out for everyone'.

This is the Word of the Lord.
R. Thanks be to God.

Sing 'Meals we share' *(Rejoice 1 No. 40)*

Discussion

Where did Jesus and his friends go for their special meal?
What food and drink did they have?
What did Jesus do before they ate and drank?
What did he say to them about the bread and wine?

Explanation

At Mass, the priest does what Jesus did.

The people bring the bread and wine to the altar, with the money they give to support the Church.

The priest puts the bread and wine on the altar and invites us to give thanks to God for all his gifts. He says 'Let us give thanks to the Lord our God' and we all say 'It is right to give him thanks and praise'.

The priest says the words of Jesus. 'Take this all of you and eat it: this is my body, which will be given up for you. This is the cup of my blood. It will be shed for you and for all.' The bread and wine become Jesus.

3 REFLECTION (5 mins)

God our loving Father,
we are glad to give you thanks and praise
because you love us.
With Jesus we sing your praise

R. Glory to God in the highest
or Hosanna in the highest.

Because you love us
you gave us this great and beautiful world
with Jesus we sing your praise. **R.**

Because you love us
you sent Jesus your Son
to bring us to you
and to gather us round him
as the children of one family
with Jesus we sing your praise. **R.**

Invite some of the children to share their LITANY OF THANKS AND PRAISE with us, then to place them in an appropriate place.

4 GOODBYES

- Thank everyone for coming along.
- Remind them of the date of the next session.
- The catechists will stay on to answer any questions that people might have.
- Ask the children to share the panel with their parents.

GO OUT

Before you begin

Material to be used by Catechists prior to Session 4 **GO OUT**

What we hope to achieve

To begin to understand the concept of stewardship.
To recognise those who support us in this task
and those whom we can support.

1 LOOKING AT OUR LIVES

Our role as catechists is to share our faith and to nurture the faith of our young people. Share together your experience of working with these children over the last few weeks. What was good? Why? What was difficult? Why? What would we consider to be the important values, skills and attitudes we have tried to foster with these children?

Play some quiet music. Listen as someone reads Interview with God .

Interview with God

'Come in,' said God. 'So you would like to interview Me?'

'If you have the time,' I said.

God smiled and said, 'My time is eternity and is enough to do everything. What questions do you have in mind to ask me?'

'What surprises you most about humanity?'

God answered:

'That they get bored of being children, are in a rush to grow up and then long to be children again.

That they lose their health to make money and then lose their money to restore their health.

That by thinking anxiously about the future, they forget the present, such that they live neither for the present nor for the future.

That they live as if they will never die, and they die as if they had never lived…'

God took my hands in His and we were silent for a while.

(pause)

Then I asked: 'As a parent, what are some of life's lessons you want your children to learn?'

God replied with a smile,

'To learn that they cannot make anyone love them. What they can do is to let themselves be loved...

To learn that what is most valuable is not what they have in their lives, but who they have in their lives.

To learn that it is not good to compare themselves with others. All will be judged individually on their own merits, not as a group on a comparison basis.

To learn that a rich person is not the one who has the most, but is the one who needs the least.

To learn that it takes only a few seconds to open profound wounds in persons we love, and that it takes many years to heal them.

To learn forgiveness by practising it.

To learn that there are persons who love them dearly, but simply do not know how to express or show their feelings.

To learn that money can buy everything but happiness.

To learn that two people can look at the same thing and see it totally differently.

To learn that a true friend is someone who knows everything about them – and loves them anyway.

To learn that it is not always enough they be forgiven by others, but that they have to forgive themselves.

To learn that people will forget what you said, people will forget what you did, but people will never forget how you made them feel.'

I thanked God for His time and for all that he had done for me and for those whom I love, and He replied, 'Anytime. I'm here twenty-four hours a day. Ask for me and I'll answer.'

(Provenance unknown but received in e-mail form from a friend who got it from a friend...)

You may like to share this with parents after the final celebration together. This links with the "hopes and dreams" they shared together in their second session together.

To think about and discuss

Which sentence speaks most to you? Why?
What is there in the reflections that could influence how we live our lives in future?
What would your response be?

2a LOOKING AT GOD'S WORD

Go out all over the world based on Matthew 28:16-20

Now the eleven disciples went to Galilee, to the mountain to which Jesus had directed them. When they saw him, they worshipped him; but some doubted. And Jesus came and said to them, "All authority in heaven and on earth has been given to me. Go therefore and make disciples of all nations, baptizing them in the name of the Father and of the Son and of the Holy Spirit, and teaching them to obey everything that I have commanded you. And remember, I am with you always, to the end of the age."

This is the Word of the Lord.
R. Thanks be to God.

b LOOKING AT OUR RESPONSE

What is it that we are being called to do?
What demands does this make of us?
What difficulties can we foresee, if any?
Who could help us?
How can we support each other?

How can we help the children in our parish discover what it means to 'Go in peace to love and serve the Lord'?

3 MAKING CONNECTIONS

During Session 4 we are going to help the children do this through an exploration of:

- the ministry of the key person(s) – Special Minister of Holy Communion
- the meaning and use of the key objects – the chalice, paten, pyx (very special vessels);
- the meaning of the key location – the open door – reminding us that we 'go out";
- The meaning of the key phrases – 'Peace be with you – and also with you' and 'Go in peace to love and serve the Lord'.

Ideas for the display

Cover a small table with a cloth. Place a chalice, a paten and a pyx on the table.

Children's Session 4 **GO OUT**

What we hope to achieve

To begin to understand the concept of service.
To recognise those who support us in this task
and those whom we can support.

Key person/people – **Special Minister of Holy Communion**

Key phrase – '**Go in peace to love and serve the Lord.'**

'Thanks be to God.'

Key object – **pyx**

Key place – **open door**

Use pictures from the back of this book to help explore these key elements

1 WELCOME AND INTRODUCTION (10 mins)

During this final session we are going to think about what happens when we have finished celebrating Mass. We are asked to 'Go in peace to love and serve the Lord'. During Mass we offer each other a sign of this peace. One person says 'Peace be with you' and the other person replies 'And also with you'.

Offer each other the Sign of Peace

Working around the display

- What is here?
- What do you think it is used for?
- Have you ever seen it being used before? When? How?

Key person

Explain who the (key person) will be:
What kind of questions would they like to ask them?

The catechist should write up a list and ask the group who would like to ask the various questions (be aware that some children will prefer not to). Prompt the children where necessary.

Prompt questions for use with the key person:

- How did you become a Eucharistic Minister?
- How did you become involved in the work you do?
- Why do you do it?
- If you were asked – how did you feel?
- How much time does your job take?
- Did you have special training?
- What does your work in church involve?
- Do you have instructions you need to follow?
- What happens when you take Holy Communion to a sick or housebound person?
- What special equipment do you use?
- Do you need to be a certain age to do this work?
- How often do you do this work – daily, weekly, occasionally?
- Do you enjoy your role?
- Do you need special clothes?

2 ACTIVITIES (20 mins)

STORY ***The Rainbow Fish*** by Marcus Pfisteras Wood
(Published by Walker Books ISBN 1-55858-009-3)

Synopsis

In this story we are introduced to a beautiful fish with many silvery scales. As he swims in the ocean another fish asks for one of the scales. At first the Rainbow fish refuses. The other fish do not want to share their time with the Rainbow Fish. He becomes very lonely and unhappy. He seeks advice but doesn't like the advice he is given as this means he would have to share.

Making the connections between the story and the key person

One of the most important things we are asked to do as Christians is to 'Love one another, as I have loved you'. John 13:34.

In this story the Rainbow Fish unselfishly gives of itself to others in need. As members of the Church there are many tasks we are able to undertake to bear witness to God's love. The role of the Eucharistic Minister is one of these.

How the story fits in

Each person has been given different gifts and talents. This story encourages children to 'Go Out' to love and serve the Lord using their unique gifts or talents. By doing this we bear witness to God's love and enrich the lives of others.

'You give little when you give of your possessions. It is when you give of yourself you truly give'. (Kahlil Gibran)

Eventually he reluctantly gives away one of the scales and realises there is a 'feel good' factor to sharing with others. This sharing continues until he only has one scale left. However, the Rainbow fish realises he has become much happier by sharing with others.

Read the story

Key questions

How well did you listen to the story?
What made the Rainbow fish look beautiful?
Why didn't the Rainbow fish want to share his scales?

3 KEY PERSON (15 mins)

The catechist facilitates the encounter, encouraging the children to ask questions. Use the prompt questions with the children to interview the key person.

The Eucharistic Minister introduces the children to the key phrase and location.

Ask the Eucharistic Minister to role-play what happens when he/she visits the sick or housebound. Let some of the group take a role e.g. the sick person, a member of the family, the priest who sends the Eucharistic Minister out from church to visit part of the church community.

4 CLOSING DOWN (10 mins)

Think of one thing you could do to 'Love and Serve the Lord in Peace'.
Invite the children to write or draw what they have thought about on a 'card'.
Light a candle. Ask the children to place their card in a basket and if they wish, say what they have put on the card. Thank God for all the good the children will do when they 'go out'. These will be taken to the celebration.

Celebration to follow Session 4 **GO OUT**

1 GATHERING (5 mins)

- Welcome the parents as they join the children for this final session.
- Thank them for coming each week and ask about how everyone is looking forward to the First Communion Celebrations.
- Gather them close to the altar.
- Quickly recap previous celebrations and special visitors.
- On this final week we can come to the Open Door.

Recap the children's session

- What was our story about this week?
- Who is our Special Visitor this week?
- What did you like best about what (Eucharistic Minister's name) told you?
- Would anyone like to be a Eucharistic Minister when they get a bit older? Why?

2 SCRIPTURE READING (10 mins)

Introduce: The Eucharistic Minister has a very special role in the parish particularly when they take communion to the sick. The priest/or deacon says at the end of Mass 'Let us go in peace to love and serve the Lord.' We say 'Thanks be to God.' The Eucharistic Minister goes out to serve the sick and housebound, what do we do to love and serve the Lord? Listen to this story of what Jesus said to his disciples.

Light the Gospel Candle

Sing an Alleluia song e.g. 'Halle, halle, halle' or 'Pass it On!' *(Rejoice One, No. 71)*

Read *(The special person could read)*

Go out all over the world based on Matthew 28:16-20

The eleven disciples set out for Galilee, to the mountain where Jesus had said he would meet them. When they saw him they knelt down before him. Jesus said to them, 'My Father had given me power in heaven and on earth. Go all over the whole world. Make disciples of all the peoples. Baptise, them, in the name of the Father and of the Son and of the Holy Spirit. Teach everyone to live as I have taught you how to live; show everyone how to love as I have shown you how to love. Remember my promise. I am with you always, close by, ready to help, yes, for ever until the very end of time.'

This is the Word of the Lord.
R. Thanks be to God.

Sing 'Go out' *(Rejoice One No. 72)*

Discussion

Where did Jesus say he would meet his disciples?
What else did he say to the woman?
Have you heard the priest say anything like this at Mass?
When he met his disciples, what did he tell them to do?
Did he want them to stay at home and keep quiet?
What does the Eucharistic Minister do when he/she goes our from the Church?
What can we do to bring peace and love to people when we go out from Church?

Explanation

Today we are thinking about the open door of the Church, about what happens when we go out.

Jesus gave his disciples a message of peace, and he wants the whole world to know about it.

The Eucharistic Minister takes holy communion to those who cannot come to Church because they are sick: this is bringing them Jesus himself, with his message of peace.

We can tell other people about Jesus and his message of love and peace.

We can show people how to love, by the way we live.

3 REFLECTION (5 mins)

Let's gather our thoughts as we come to the end of our preparation time and look forward to the celebration when you will receive Jesus for the first time in HOLY COMMUNION.

We are thankful for the many 'special visitors' we have met who have told us about their ministry in the Church especially today's special visitor (Eucharistic Minister) who takes communion to the sick. We ask God to bless them and all those that they help.

> God Our Father,
> we have come close to you
> and your Son Jesus during
> our time together.
> Guide us as we take your message
> of peace to all we meet and help us to
> grow in your love and service.
> Amen.

> As we go through this door today
> May the Lord
> be in our minds
> on our lips
> and in our hearts
> now and forever.

4 GOODBYES

- Thank everyone for coming along.
- Practical arrangements about the days of celebration.
- Invite children to share panel (if approriate).
- Give parents their copy of "Interview with God".

Celebrations

Time and place

In the church immediately following on from the catechetical session.

In the same space in which the catechesis took place immediately following on from the catechetical session.

Focal points

- If the celebration takes place in the church building, then the children and their families gather with the catechists at the location designated within the celebration plan for each session.
- If the celebration takes place in the same place as the catechetical session, then the children and their families gather with the catechists around the display.

Gathering

- If the celebration takes place in church immediately after the catechetical session, then the parents could gather in the church building towards the end of the catechetical session. It would be important that a member of the catechetical team should be there to greet them – this is a useful time for parents to ask practical questions about the preparation process and First Communion day itself.
- Similarly, if the celebration takes place in the room used for catechesis immediately after the catechetical session, then it is preferable to have a catechist available to greet the parents as they arrive and – if possible – meet together with them in a different space to that used for catechesis. Remember – early arriving parents can prove a distraction to their children!
- If the celebration takes place at a later date to the catechetical session, then the parents gather with their children inside the space and around the focal point.

Picture resource

The pictures on the following pages can be used to illustrate the parents' and children's sessions where it is difficult to obtain or display the items.

The display panel shown below is an additional resource for the children and provides a link between home and parish and also, when the centre panel is completed, a memento of their First Communion.

BLESSED ARE THEY THAT MOURN
BLESSED ARE THE PURE IN HEART

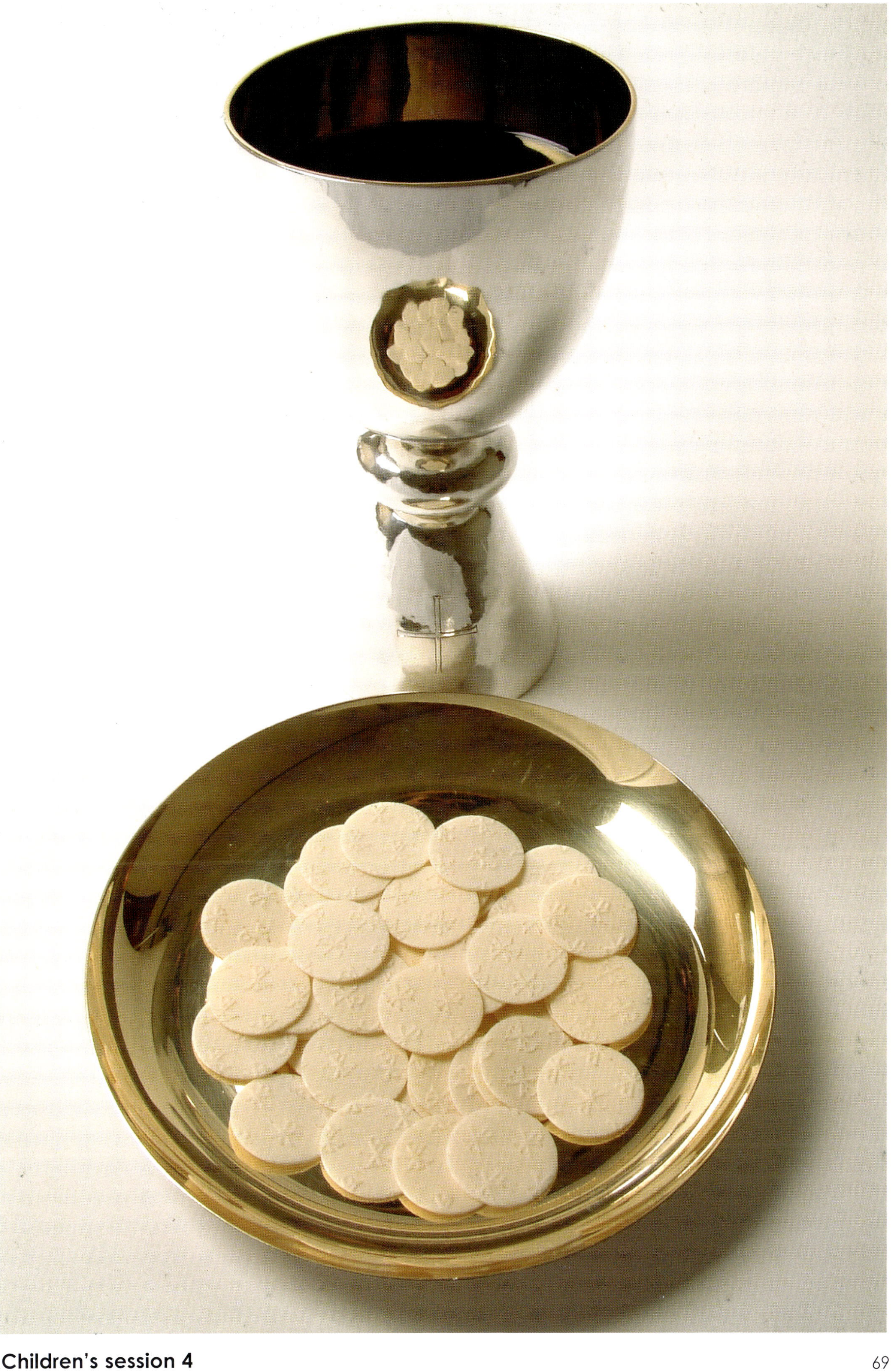

IHS